GREAT RAILWAY
PHOTOGRAPHERS

E. R. WETHERSETT

Presented by Colin Garratt
from the collections of the National Railway Museum

This edition first published in 1996 by Milepost Publishing in association with
Arcturus Publishing Limited

for

Selectabook
Folly Road, Roundway, Devizes, Wilts. SN10 2HR

Milepost Publishing is a division of Milepost 92¹/₂
Colin Garratt's audio-visual/video production,
photographic service and picture library for the railway industry.
Milepost also conserves and markets historic collections of negatives and transparencies

Designed by Milepost and Just My Type.

Printed and bound in Great Britain

ISBN 1 900193 65 5

Milepost 92¹/₂
Newton Harcourt
Leicestershire
LE8 9FH
Tel 0116 2592068

MILEPOST

PREVIOUS PAGE : *A down express passing Cemetery signal box hauled by ex Great Central Railway War Memorial locomotive, L.N.E.R. Class B3/1, No. 6165 "Valour" (587)*

INTRODUCTION
by Colin Garratt

Ernest Richard Wethersett was born in 1893 and died on the 3rd of October 1987 at the age of 94, having enjoyed a longevity similar to that of many other leading railway photographers.

He had personal links with such celebrated names as E.Pouteau and F.E.Mackay. E.R.W. was a member of the Stephenson Locomotive Society for some 50 years. David Bayes, writing in the S.L.S. journal in March/April 1988 said: "E.R.W. was generous in build and in nature. Modest and taciturn but with a delightful and sardonic wit. He started Bishop Treacy off with his first "real" camera after the war. His immaculate photography, with never a smudged buffer beam, will continue to delight and perpetuate the memory of this likeable man".

ABOVE : *Three of the pre-grouping railways named locomotives to commemorate the railwaymen who were killed in the 1914-18 war; the Great Central (see title page), the London and North Western and the London Brighton and South Coast. The L.B.S.C. locomotive was a Class L 4-6-4T No. 333 named "Remembrance". It is seen here at New Cross shed carrying its second Southern Railway number, applied in 1932, 2333 and in dark green livery. After electrification of the Brighton line the class was transferred to Eastbourne where they remained until electrification in 1935. There was then no more suitable work due to their limited coal and water capacity so they were rebuilt as 4-6-0 tender engines.*

I am not sure what the photographer on the left is doing but he appears to have two cameras, holding one and one on the ground! (6073)

ABOVE : *The London and North Eastern Railway gained access to Liverpool by virtue of a two thirds partnership in the Cheshire Lines Committee. (Most of whose lines were in Lancashire!) Their terminus was Central Station, the high level portion of which is now raised to the ground although the former Mersey Railway underground station has been rebuilt and serves the electrified Merseyrail system. The locomotive shed was at Brunswick some miles out of Central through some very murky tunnels and hard by the Dingle terminus of the Liverpool overhead Railway.*

Seen outside the shed in about 1947 are L.N.E.R. Class D9, 4-4-0 No. 2315, Class B1, 4-6-0 No. 1036 "Ralph Asheton" and possibly another D9

E.R.Wethersett apparently used two cameras as there is a quarter plate or 5"x 4" reflex on the ground, extreme right. (2294).

E.R.W. lived near Willesden Junction with his wife; they had no children and he worked as a factotum in the Royal Courts of Justice.

E.R.W. was active in railway photography from 1918 until 1960. His negatives are all on glass plate, 3 1/4 X 4 1/4, and the legacy is believed to total around 2,500 pictures all of which are now held by the National Railway Museum. Brian Stephenson in cataloguing E.R.W.'s work has located the highest negative numbers on pictures made at Swindon on 16.10.60 and has drawn the reasonable conclusion that this was the last date on which E.R.W. took photographs.

E.R.W. was essentially an L.N.E.R. photographer, concentrating particularly on the southern reaches of the East Coast Main Line. He was friendly with B.Atkinson, the shed foreman at Kings Cross during the 1930s and had virtually free access to the depot. This friendship also enabled him to gain access to other parts of the L.N.E.R. system. With this privilege he worked quietly and unassumingly, sometimes in the company of Charles Gordon Stuart who, having inherited a fortune, didn't need to work and devoted his time to photography on an amateur level and visiting railways worldwide. Compared with many other leading railway photographers E.R.W. worked little beyond the Greater London area although he did work on the southern parts of the West Coast and Midland Main Lines.

E.R.W. was meticulous in setting his pictures up and tenacious in striving to achieve the exact results he wanted. The essential Wethersett was a classic "Front Three Quarter" view, with big skies and open landscape. This approach describes 90% of his work although he was attracted by pictorial aids like viaducts, tunnels, water troughs and the transformation of the landscape brought about by snow. His pictures are usually taken from "safe and predictable" vantage points. In this respect he was different to that other great photographer of the L.N.E.R. C.C.B.Herbert, whose pictures reveal a much wider variety of vantage points and angles - aided no doubt by the fact that Herbert was an L.N.E.R employee. E.R.W.'s endless views of the East Coast Main Line show detail variations on themes which enabled him, in the fullness of time, to capture the ultimate shot resulting in some of the finest pictures of the L.N.E.R. ever recorded.

BELOW : *The London Tilbury and Southend section of the L.M.S. relied on 4-4-2Ts for its passenger service until the advent of Stanier's 3 cylinder 2-6-4Ts in 1935. Some of the 4-4-2Ts lingered on until BR days and two are seen here looking much the worse for wear and awaiting scrapping. The location may be Tilbury shed before it was rebuilt in the mid 1960s. The L.T.S. was a Westinghouse brake line but the older stock was withdrawn and replaced by L.M.S. vacuum brake stock, the locomotives lost their air pumps, as has this one. (2562)*

ABOVE : *The main line out of Euston was always popular with photographers and there were a number of convenient vantage points. This is Kilburn High Road station between Willesden and Camden, some three miles out of Euston.*

A down evening local bound for Bletchley or Northampton is on the down fast line hauled by an ex L.N.W.R. "Experiment "class 4-6-0. The line was widened here for the 1922 electrification to Euston and the two fast lines furthest from the camera were on a new alignment. The slow lines in the foreground were the former fast lines and the former slow lines, off the picture to the left, became the D.C. electric lines. Up to 1917, Kilburn High Road was served by steam trains and there was the down fast line platform where the bushes are between the present fast and slow lines. These four lines were electrified on the 25kV A.C. overhead system in the mid 60s. (433)

His ouvre includes many exotic pictures for which there was not space in this volume; the L.M.S. Turbomotive, running light over Bushey troughs; Ivatt Atlantics on the East Coast Main Line on the snowy Christmas Eve of 1937 and an un-rebuilt Royal Scot, seen through the chimneys of a North London maisonette in the 1940s.

During his last years of photography, he spent many weeks in Hove with his friend J.E.Kite photographing the surviving L.B.&S.C.R. locomotives.

Few shed scenes are found in his work; few locomotive portraits and few freights. He was attracted to the biggest and latest; A3s, A4s, Royal Scots, Princess Royals, Duchesses. He seemed to have little interest in recording vintage engines on rural by-ways and, by the same token, industrial engines do not feature in his work at all. Again, he contrasts with C.C.B.Herbert, who stated "The natural tendency to concentrate on pictures of the newest and largest is to be resisted". Working in the 20s and 30s, the amount of ancient types available to E.R.W. would have been incredible but he simply didn't

LEFT, below : *In July 1937 the L.M.S. introduced a high speed streamlined train "The Coronation Scot" which covered the 401 miles from Euston to Glasgow in 6^{1}/2 hours. Five streamlined 4-6-2 locomotives were built to run this train and other heavy West Coast services. Here the first of the class No. 6220 "Coronation" is being shunted into platform 6 at Euston for a press preview in June 1937.*
The shunting locomotive is an ex L.N.W.R 0-6-0 No.8442 colloquially known as "Cauliflowers" from the L.N.W.R. armorial device carried on the centre splasher prior to 1923 which looked like the aforementioned vegetable!
The locomotive and train names celebrated the coronation of King George VI which was held on 12the May 1937. (1314)

ABOVE : *Former L.N.W.R. "Prince of Wales" Class 4-6-0 No.5678 "Milton" around the back of Willesden Locomotive Depot, probably in the early 1930s. Milton carries an L.N.W.R. style shedplate on the smokebox door (No.2 was Willesden). Note the very ornate oil lamp on the right.*

photograph them. The latest and most powerful was to pre-occupy him for the whole of his photographic career, and by 1960 had manifested in such types as the Britannias and Clan pacifics. One feels that the superb rendition of the L.and N.W. "Cauliflower" alongside would never have been taken had it not been for the new, streamlined "Coronation" pacific, which the veteran 0-6-0 has in tow.

E.R.W. belonged to a fine and noble tradition of railway photographers who insisted that the whole train should appear in a picture. The train was always the main concern; infrastructure, topography, the density and complexity of the railway with its stations, sidings, and related industry are omitted. In fact, most of E.R.W.s pictures could have been taken on today's vastly shrunken network. His use of telegraph poles and signals is invariably well chosen and imaginative. He also tended to follow the simplistic rule of "framing" the train with some tangible object placed either side of it; signals, a tree, buildings or whatever.

There can be few greater contrasts in railway photographic technique than Henry Priestley's diverse topographical scenes featuring hum drum trains set amid the diversity of the railway infrastructure and its surrounds and E.R.W.'s flamboyant expresses set in wide open spaces. But E.R.W.seems to have had little feeling for the posterity element in his work; he obviously enjoyed his hobby, portraying trains in the way he felt most inclined to do.

Within two years of finishing photography E.R.W. gave his entire collection to the Ian Allan organisation for use in their books and magazines. Subsequently, six hundred of these, dating from 1921 to1934, were issued, by Ian Allan, as post cardsized prints at 2/6d each under the general title "The E.R.Wethersett Collection". It seems that this first batch was not sufficiently successful commercially and no later set was issued. It is an interesting reflection that the legacy was given to Ian Allan 25 years before E.R.W.'s death.

He was deeply disturbed by the passing of the steam age which robbed him of his life long love. Modern traction held no interest for him whatsoever and once the rundown of steam got under way a chapter of his life came to an abrupt end.

E.R.W.'s collection was purchased by the National Railway Museum with assistance from the National Heritage Memorial Fund as part of the Ian Allan collection in the early 1990s. There was very little in the way of written notes and the captions for this volume have been provided by John Edgington who was formally the Technical Information Officer at the National Railway Museum. John, who began as a professional railway man with the L.M.S. in 1942, has an all round knowledge of railways matched by few individuals living today and I am much indebted to him.

Many of E.R.W.'s pictures are ultimate manifestations in their own right. Page 35 shows a Gresley A3 caught at a magical angle which captures the sheer beauty of these locomotives. The A4 heading the "Flying Scotsman" on page 16 seems to represent how every one would like to remember this, "the world's most famous train". The picture of Welwyn Viaduct (page 46) has a lovely thirties poster-like feel about it which catches the magic of the railway age; no less powerful is the spread on pages 32/33 showing the Forth Bridge superbly taken with the trains ultimately framed, whilst his views of the smoky exits from Kings Cross on pages 26/27 rank - alongside the work of C.C.Herbert - as the finest pictures ever made of that magnificent section of railway.

E.R.W's pictures will be enjoyed by many generations to come; his well practised compositions have an enduring quality and herein lies his intrinsic strength.

Many thanks to the National Railway Museum for providing access to the largest photographic archive in Britain. Milepost also wish to thank the staff at the N.R.M. who are involved in this series.

Colin Garratt,
Milepost 92^1/$_2$,
Newton Harcourt,
Leicestershire,
September 1996

9

ABOVE : *An up express on the Great Eastern section of the London and North Eastern Railway. The locomotive is a Class B17, 3 cylinder 4-6-0 No.2817 "Ford Castle". This class was built specifically for the Great Eastern section due to weight restrictions on some bridges. They also ran with short six wheeled tenders which would fit on the existing turntables. The train consists of ex Great Eastern corridor coaches with two restaurant cars carrying roof boards at number four and five. (875)*

A page of personalities.

PREVIOUS PAGE, above : *William Oswold Skeat B.Sc (Eng), C.Eng., F.I.Mech E., the gentleman on the left, was probably not so well known as he should have been as he was of a retiring nature. A Premium Apprentice at Doncaster he had held a number of posts in the railway and engineering world and for the last 19 years of his career was Secretary and Editor to the Institute of Water Engineers. His principal love was the Great Eastern Railway and whilst acting in his professional capacity he was able to organise a special train from London to Driffield for the I.W.E. to inspect a treatment plant there. It was, of course, hauled by a Great Eastern locomotive, albeit an L.N.E.R. rebuilt Class B12/3, 4-6-0 No. 61577. It is seen here at Lincoln Central. The gentleman by the cab looking to the right, may be John Scholes, the former curator of Historical Relics, B.T.C. (3195)*

PREVIOUS PAGE, below :
Oswald Stevens Nock B.Sc., A.M.I.C.E., M.I.Mech E., A.I.LOCO.E. was a prolific writer and probably has more railway books to his name than any other author. Here he is alongside one of the first ten L.N.E.R. Class B1, 4-6-0s No.8307 about to undertake a footplate trip which he described in one of his early books "British Locomotives at Work". The journey was from Ipswich to March on the 6.45am Colchester to York in July 1945. The photographer is probably at Ipswich where Locomotives were changed and the B1 took over. (1827)

ABOVE : *The East Coast Main Line in the outskirts of London with Class A3, 4-6-2 No.2505 "Cameronian" on a down express.*

The photographer obviously chose this location with care as there was a temporary speed restriction for re-sleepering on the down fast line, witness the new sleepers lying in the "six foot" and the ballast removed from the down fast. This and other photographs were probably taken without looking through the viewfinder at the time of exposure. Note how the train is carefully placed between the telegraph pole and the short post on the right. (1231)

BELOW : *A down local train just north of Finsbury Park station. The park itself is on the left of the picture and the bridge gives access to Hornsey Gate into Finsbury Park and to Endyman Road. The locomotive is "Silver Fox", a Class A4, 4-6-2, but it is so filthy that it is impossible to read the number. I suspect that it has been re-numbered 17 so we can date the picture as winter 1946/7, probably after the heavy snow of that winter had disappeared. (2065)*

Two views of Audley End Tunnel

ABOVE : *Audley End and Littlebury Tunnels on the Liverpool Street to Cambridge main line are little more than covered ways and normally cuttings would have sufficed . They were built at the insistence of Lord Braybrook of Audley End Mansion on whose land they occurred. He was also responsible for their ornate portals.*

Ex G.E. Class B12, 4-6-0 No. 8522 leaves the south portal of Audley End Tunnel with an up express. The headcode on the locomotive is designated by white disks rather than headlamps as was the practice on other sections of the L.N.E.R. (466)

ABOVE : *Potters Bar tunnel with a down express hauled by Class A3, 4-6-2 No. 4480 "Enterprise" . No. 4480 was built at Doncaster in April 1925 as a Class A1 locomotive with a boiler pressed to 180 lbs per square inch and short travel valves. The class was not entirely satisfactory and "Enterprise" was rebuilt in July 1927 to Class A3 with a 220 lb per square inch pressure boiler and long travel valves. This did the trick and further new 4-6-2s were built as Class A3 and eventually all the Class A1 was rebuilt to confirm. This was a long drawn out process, and the last one converted, No. 68 "Sir Visto" was not done until December 1948. The leading coach appears to be what the L.N.E.R. described as a 'Vestibule Locker Third', i.e. it was a seven compartment corridor third with a luggage locker or small van at one end. This can be seen in the picture and it has no windows and no guard's door with drop light. The colour light signal has only recently been brought into use and is automatic, i.e. controlled by track circuits and returned to danger by the passing of the train into the next section, as denoted by the white oblong plate with horizontal black band. (1339)*

LEFT, below : *The same location in May 1936 with an up coal train hauled by a Class J39, 0-6-0 No. 2726. This locomotive was one of twenty built in 1928/9 for the Great Eastern section and was fitted with Westinghouse air brakes. As No. 2726 was a Stratford engine the train had probably originated at March, but the coal would have come either from Yorkshire or Derbyshire via the Great Northern - Great Eastern Joint line to March. (23892)*

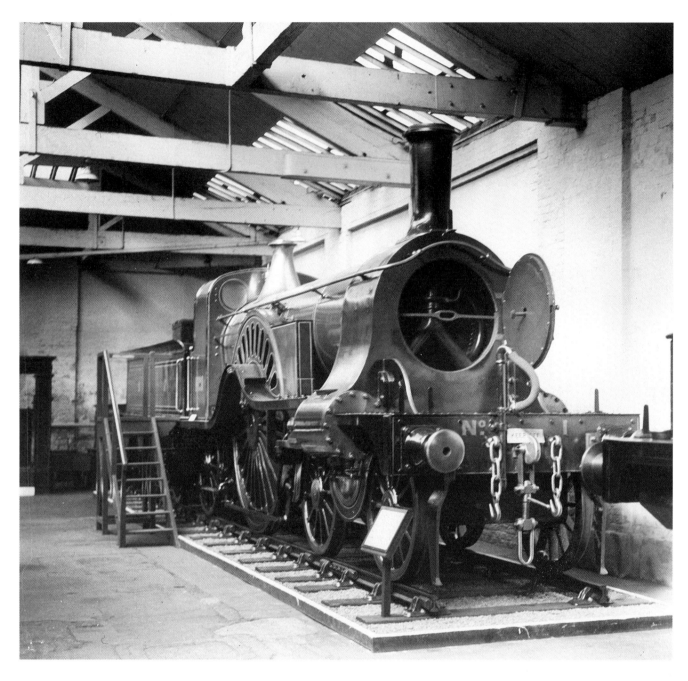

ABOVE :The London and North Eastern Railway Museum at York (Queen Street) in the 1930s with Great Northern Railways 4-2-2 locomotive No.1 built at Doncaster in 1870. The North Eastern Railway had been collecting relics for some years prior to 1922 which were housed in the basement of the HQ offices. In that year a committee was formed to find a more suitable building in which to display the collection. The old machine shop at the famous Queen Street locomotive works, closed in 1905, was selected. The Stockton and Darlington Centenary in 1925 was the catalyst for enlarging the collection and after the celebrations were over, the exhibits from Darlington were moved to Queen Street. The museum was at first open only to invited guests and by appointment. It would appear that it was open to the general public from early 1928. Over the years items from railways other than the L.N.E.R. were donated to the museum. After the formation of BR, a museum was also created in a former L.T. tram/bus garage at Clapham. This and the Queen Street collection closed in 1973 and the whole formed the nucleus of the National Railway Museum opened in 1975. (1343)

ABOVE : *In addition to their main workshops, railways had smaller premises attached to locomotive sheds where quite heavy repairs could be carried out. This is the Great Western's repair shop at Old Oak Common, London. Amongst the locomotives visible are two 2-4-0Ts with brackets to hold destination boards for London suburban trains. (534)*

A4s in Action
ABOVE : *The cliff top north of Berwick-upon-Tweed is the setting for the down "Flying Scotsman" hauled by No. 4487 "Sea Eagle". The locomotive was at first painted green but is seen here in the blue livery applied in February 1938. The coaches appear to be those specially built for this train in 1938 and include a "triplet" restaurant car (a three coach articulated set on four bogies permanently coupled. (23817)*

BELOW : *An up express behind No. 4484 "Falcon" emerges from Welwyn South tunnel c. 1935. The locomotive is in the blue livery applied in December 1937. The train appears to be fairly nondescript as there is a six wheeled van next to the engine. (23814)*

ABOVE :*The Royal Border Bridge at Berwick-upon-Tweed opened by Queen Victoria on 29 August 1850. Rather surprisingly the River Tweed here is not the boundary between England and Scotland although Berwick is more Scottish than English. The boundary is some three miles north of Berwick and marked by a sign erected by the L.N.E.R. The up Coronation is crossing the bridge hauled by one of the five dedicated A4s allocated to this train, No. 4489 "Dominion of Canada". No. 4489 was presented with a Canadian railway type bell by the Canadian Pacific Railway on 11 March 1938 which was mounted in front of the chimney. This photograph must, therefore, have been taken in the summer of 1937 as there is no bell. The train consists of the summer formation of four articulated pairs of coaches plus the "Beaver Tail" observation car. (1383)*

A Trio of L.M.S. Trains

ABOVE : *The top of Camden bank one mile from Euston. A down express passes Camden loco shed hauled by an ex-London and North Western Railway "Claughton" Class 4-6-0. Although probably seven or eight years into the "grouping" era. Apart from the livery the train is almost 100% L.N.W. The signal box just behind the locomotive is Camden No.1, an L.N.W. gantry type box which was replaced by an L.M.S. Air Raid precaution box of brick with a concrete roof in 1940. (376)*

BELOW : *The down "Merseyside Express", 6.05 pm Euston to Liverpool Lime Street behind "Princess Royal" Class 4-6-2 No. 46204 "Princess Louise", somewhere "north of Watford". The train at this time consisted of 14 coaches including three for Southport which were detached at Edge Hill. Rather surprisingly the leading coach appears to be an L.N.E.R. vehicle. (3117)*

ABOVE : *An unidentified "Royal Scot" 4-6-0 on a down express passing milepost 17 between Bushey and Watford. The train's reporting number is W119 which may be a late afternoon departure from Euston, possibly 4.0pm or thereabouts. The reporting numbers were invaluable to signal men but they obstructed the locomotive's smoke box number plate! This was probably taken about 1946 as the train is a heavy one of 13 coaches and there is no sign of a restaurant car. (1666)*

ABOVE : *A scene on England's earliest cross-country line (literally), the Newcastle & Carlisle, opened in 1836. A local train from Carlisle hauled by Class B1, 4-6-0 No. 1219 passing milepost 7 from Newcastle between Rylan and Wylam. The photograph can be dated between July 1947 when the engine was new and September 1948 when it was renumbered 61219. Note the delightful N.E.R. slotted post distant signal. (23520)*

BELOW : *The Great Central Railway was the last main line to enter London, in 1899, and it did so in part by joint ownership with the Metropolitan via Harrow and the Great Western via High Wycombe. An ex-Great Central Class A5, 4-6-2T No. 69821 is at the head of a six coach train on the G.W & G.C. joint line early in B.R. days. 69821 was renumbered in February 1919. (23597)*

ABOVE : *The down "Yorkshire Pullman" leaves Hadley North tunnel behind Class A4 4-6-2 No. 60003 "Andrew K McCosh" in the mid 50s. The train was a heavy one consisting of eleven Pullman cars with portions for Hull (detached at Doncaster), Bradford and Harrogate which split at Leeds. (23533)*

BELOW : *The post war down Flying Scotsman near the Scottish border. The locomotive is Class A3 No.65 "Knight of Thistle". The name is incorrect as the locomotive was originally named "Knight of the Thistle". The definite article was dropped in December 1932 making a nonsense of the name. The stock is all of post-war Thompson design except for the triplet restaurant car set. (23635)*

ABOVE : *On the Great Eastern section Cambridge main line near Whittlesford Class B17, 4-6-0 No. "Wynyard Park" on a down express. (750)*

ABOVE : *The Great Central section of the L.N.E.R. also ran trains over the Met & G.C. joint line from Marylebone to Aylesbury and beyond terminating at such stations as Brackley. Class A5, 4-6-2T No. 5452 is seen at Dutchlands with a six coach train. (1627x)*

LEFT, below : *The Metropolitan Railway operated an outer-suburban train to Aylesbury and (until 1936) to Verney Junction and by virtue of these trains considered itself to be a "Main Line Railway". The Aylesbury trains were hauled by electric locomotives from Baker Street and the City in rush hours, to Rickmansworth (from 1925, prior to this Harrow) where a quick exchange was made to steam traction. The L.N.E.R. took over the working of these trains north of Rickmansworth on 1 November 1937. Metropolitan Class K 2-6-4T No. 116 is seen near Dutchlands between July 1933, when the Met became part of London Transport, and 1937. This was the last steam locomotive built for the Met and was erected by Sir W. G. Armstrong-Whitworth Ltd from parts manufactured at Woolwich Arsenal with boilers built by Robert Stephenson & Co. at Darlington. This class was nominally a freight locomotive and it was unusual to find one on a passenger train. (23775)*

The "Northern Belle" was a cruise train similar to today's "Royal Scotsman". The itinerary lasted one week from Friday e commencing Friday 23 June 1939. There were usually three tours each summer in late May and June. Sixty passengers sleeping cars. For the last four seasons the itinerary was mainly on Scottish lines including, with the co-operation of the L 4467 "Wild Swan", which was new in February 1938. See the front cover picture of Wild Swan in its post-war guise and c

ng departure from Kings Cross to the following Friday morning. The service started in June 1933 and the last train ran
r train were conveyed at a cost of £20 each. The composition of the train was 14 vehicles, six of which were first class
S., a visit to Inverness. One of 1938 or 1939 trains is seen leaving Kings Cross (platform 10) behind class A4 4-6-2, No.
ing the new number 21, under the 1946 renumbering scheme.) (23811)

ABOVE : *The Class V2, 2-6-2s were a true mixed traffic locomotive being used on freight trains and the less important express trains. No. 4813 is leaving Gas Works tunnel Kings Cross with a modest down express in 1939. No. 4813 was allocated to New England (Peterborough) when new. The up coal train on the far track, the up slow, must be destined for the Southern Railway via the Metropolitan Widened Lines and Ludgate Hill. It consists of wagons owned by collieries and coal merchants (large and small) plus one stranger, BQC Clee Hill Quarries. How that came to be loaded with coal for the Southern we will never know! (23844).*

BELOW : *The down Yorkshire Pullman, 4.45pm Kings Cross to Bradford, Harrogate and Hull, hauled by Class A4 No. 4499. This locomotive was originally named "Pochard" when new, but was renamed "Sir Murrough Wilson", deputy Chairman of the L.N.E.R., and given stainless steel cut out numbers and letters in April 1939. It is seen here with the new nameplate covered but there is no record of an official naming ceremony. The locomotive on the left is of interest being the first large boiler 4-4-2 of the G.N.R. and now preserved at the National Railway Museum. (2382)*

In the 1930s, the L.N.E.R. held a number of exhibitions of locomotives and rolling stock in goods yards around the country but particularly in the London area. The proceeds were donated to charities.

ABOVE , BELOW and RIGHT, above: *Three views of the exhibition at Ilford on 2nd June 1934. Locomotives visible are Class A1, 4-6-2 No. 4472 "Flying Scotsman", now preserved, the brand new Class P2, 2-8-2 No. 2001 "Cock O' The North", a 4 wheel geared drive "Sentinel" shunter, Class D16/3, 4-4-0 No. 8900 "Claud Hamilton", a Class B17, 4-6-0 and a Class B12/3, 4-6-0.(p 28 top 827; p28 bottom 825; p29 top 826)*

The goods department's fixed hand crane is demonstrating the unloading of a container from a wagon. There are various coaches on display including a "Sentinel" steam railcar in green and cream livery. It was obviously a fine day and the event was very well supported.

PREVIOUS PAGE : *This appears to be an early Wethersett photograph, probably taken with a simple camera. It shows ex G.N.R. Class C1, 4-4-2 No. 4404 leaving platform 8 at Kings Cross with a local passenger train, probably destined for the main line or Cambridge, as it is in the main line station. The locomotive is in the early L.N.E.R. livery with the number on the tender. The coaches are not clear in the photograph but they appear to be two old six wheeled bodies mounted on three 4 wheeled bogies. (103)*

BELOW : *A similar event at Romford on 5the June 1936. The weather was not so brilliant but there were neverthe-less plenty of spectators. Principal exhibit is Class A4, 4-6-2 No. 2512 "Silver Fox" with its casing partially open at the front to show the means of access to the smokebox. (1144)*

ABOVE : *The Great Northern Railway never owned a 4-6-0 but for 25 years until 1922 they relied on 4-4-2s. After superheating the large boiler locomotives were excellent machines and some lasted into BR days. A farewell run for the last of the class, BR No. 62822 ran from Kings Cross to Doncaster on 26the November 1950.*

The day started very foggy in London as is shown in the picture but this cleared by Grantham. The headboard was not universally admired and some photographers refused to take pictures. I hope E.R.Wethersett had a photographic permit as he is standing in the "four foot" of platform 8 at Kings Cross. (2668)

RIGHT, above : *Class C1, 4-4-2 No. 4450 on a bleak winter's day somewhere in East Anglia, maybe on the Cambridge line. The leading coach is a lavatory brake composite with three third class compartments, two firsts and a guard cum luggage van plus a lavatory for each class, a type much favoured by some railways for cross country trains and through coaches detached off expresses to serve branch lines. (1221A)*

RIGHT, below : *When Douglas Earle Marsh became Locomotive Superintendent of the London Brighton and South Coast Railway, he designed two classes of 4-4-2 locomotives which were very similar to Ivatt's large boiler Atlantics on the G.N.R. This is not surprising as Marsh came from Doncaster. The L.B.&S.C.examples lasted until the late 1950s and were favourites for the Newhaven boat trains. In their later days they were in demand for enthusiasts specials. Organised by the Railway Correspondence and Travel Society, Class H2 No. 32421 "South Foreland" worked "The Hampshireman" on 6the February 1955 from Waterloo to Guildford via Staines and Chertsey. From the "lakes" in the background the location appears to be Ashford, Middlesex between Feltham and Stains. (3038)*

Four views on the Forth Bridge

ABOVE : *It was possible even into BR days to obtain permission to photograph on the Forth Bridge although it was probably necessary for the photographer to be accompanied. The first view was taken pre-war and shows a local train from Fife hauled by ex North British Railway Class D29, 4-4-0 No. 9339 "Ivanhoe". The first coach is ex North British Railway probably a corridor third. The other four appear to be two L.N.E.R. articulated pairs and, although they are probably non-corridor, have fitting for roof mounted destination boards. (23778)*

BELOW : *Three post-war shots, all probably taken on the same day. Class V2 No. 60819 of Aberdeen is at the head of an up express, probably an Aberdeen to Edinburgh Waverley. The stock is all BR Mark1 in the first crimson and cream livery except for a pre-grouping restaurant car. (23917)*

ABOVE : *E.R.Wethersett turned round for this photograph, a down local hauled, unusually, by a Class A4, 4-6-2 No. 60004 "William Whitelaw". No. 60004 was named after the present Lord Whitelaw's grandfather who was chairman of the North British Railway. The village of South Queensferry is visible through the girders. (2495)*

BELOW : *Another down local with more usual motive power, a Class D30, 4-4-0 No. 62421 "Laird o' Monkbarns". The Class D29 and D30 locomotives were named after characters from Sir Walter Scott's novels and what wonderful and evocative names they were. (23525)*

ABOVE : *The former Great Northern Railway large "Atlantics", Class C1, were favourites for the Kings Cross to Cambridge buffet car expresses. Here, No. 4461 is seen passing through the rather featureless countryside near Royston. (864)*

ABOVE : *A post war scene just north of New Southgate with a down train hauled by probably one of the most famous Gresley Pacifics, "Flying Scotsman" by then carrying its 1946 number, 103. "Flying Scotsman" still appears to be Class A1 so the date of the photograph must be summer 1946 as it was numbered 103 in May 1946 and was rebuilt to Class A3 in January 1947. The livery should therefore have been black but No. 103 is so filthy it is impossible to tell. (23804)*

LEFT, below : *Until c.1960 the four or more tracks out of Kings Cross ended at Greenwood signal box south of Hadley Wood tunnel. Class A1, 4-6-2 No. 2550 "Blink Bonny" is heading a down morning express at Greenwood. The L.N.E.R tended to run big express trains in groups from Kings Cross with lengthy gaps between to enable freight trains to pass through the bottlenecks such as this one. The train behind "Blink Bonny" is a typical heavy one as the coaches disappear into the exhaust. Notice that E.R.Wethersett has again carefully placed the train between the signal and telegraph poles. No doubt he was watching the train and not looking through the viewfinder when he released the shutter. (23795)*

35

ABOVE : *A mystery location in Scotland. The North British Railway had a large stud of 0-6-0s to work coal traffic in Fife and the Central Lowlands. No. 64566 seen carrying its 1946 number, 4566, was a member of the most powerful class of these locomotives, the L.N.E.R. Class J37, and was rated 5F by British Railways. (2250)*

RIGHT, above : *A brief excursion to the North of England which was unusual, E.R.Wethersett mainly operated in London and the home counties and then mainly on the L.M.S. and L.N.E.R.*

The Lancashire and Yorkshire Railway operated wholly within these two counties (They had only one owned station outwith these two; Stalybridge in Cheshire)

Here is their main line across (or more literally through) the Pennines. This is approaching Sowerby Bridge, West Yorkshire, with a train of empty wagons being returned to various collieries in the county. The locomotive is an L&Y Class 31, 0-8-0 (L.M.S. Class 7F). L.M.S. No. 12857 built in 1913. The L&Y had ten sets of water troughs on its system, the highest number per route mile of any pre-grouping company. This set were known as Sowerby Bridge or Luddenfoot (the former being the official name) and No. 12857 is picking up water. (1862)

RIGHT, below:
Hessle (East Yorkshire) looking east with a westbound through freight hauled by a Class B15, 4-6-0 No. 819. The train is an enigma as the first ten or so wagons appear to be loaded with coal and, of course, there were no collieries in the Hull area.

Three photographs on the rural Southern.

ABOVE :

Ex London Brighton & South Coast Railway Class D3, 0-4-4T No. 238X (the last figure is indecipherable) is on Eastbourne duty. No. 798, which as the line is angled, is probably an Eastbourne to Hailsham local. The D3s in post-war years rarely ventured further north than Hailsham up the "Cuckoo Line". (2657)

ABOVE : *Another L.B.&S.C Class D3, No. 32379, one of the four which were re-numbered by British Railways. This one was L.B.&S.C. No. 379 named "Sanderstead". It is carrying a 75D shed plate which was Horsham and as the line is double track it must be on a Horsham to Brighton train via Steyning, confirmed by the one headcode disc in the centre of the buffer beam. The train is a two coach push and pull set of L.B.&S.C. origin. (2896A)*

LEFT, below : *The L.B.&S.C. Class A1X, 0-6-0Ts lasted until 1963 on the branch from Havant to Hayling Island. The cause of this longevity was the wooden bridge over Langston Harbour which could not carry anything heavier. No. 32661, formally L.B.&S.C. No. 61 "Sutton", is approaching Havant with a three coach train from Hayling Island. The date must be the late 1950s or after as No. 32661 is in lined black livery with the second BR crest. (3227)*

Between the tunnels at Welwyn. The up "Flying Scotsman", in the summer of either 1938 or 1939, has emerged from We the two portals for a decent length train! The locomotive is Class A4 No. 4482 "Golden Eagle" and the coaches appear to are controlled from Woolmer Green. No doubt it is impossible to take a photograph from this location today, as in man

Again the train has been accurately placed between fixed objects (23511)

North, 1047 yards long, and is about to enter the South tunnel which is 447 yards in length. There is just room between the 1938 built set with double glazing and pressure ventilation and heating. The splitting distant signals on the down line aces, due to trees obscuring the view.

ABOVE : *In 1925 Gresley introduced two large 2-8-2 locomotives specifically for working coal trains between Peterborough (New England) and London (Ferme Park). They were able to convey 100 wagons, 25% more than a 2-8-0, but this created problems finding suitable paths and, in the event, they were always rostered on specific trains with detailed instructions regarding their running.*

ABOVE : *The Great Central Railway owned a class of inside cylinder 2-6-4Ts which was unique in Britain (Class L1) and were, in fact, the only pre-grouping 2-6-4Ts apart from one on the South Eastern and Chatham.*

An unidentified member of the L.N.E. Class L1 is seen on a freight train on Denham Troughs (Great Western and Great Central Joint Line). (184)

ABOVE : *Prior to the introduction of the Class V2, 2-6-2s in 1936 the important fitted freights were worked by Class K3, 2-6-0s. No. 153 is approaching Greenwood on the 3.40pm Kings Cross Goods to Glasgow in the early 1930s. (911)*

BELOW : *The Great Eastern Railway handled quite a large tonnage of coal for London which arrived at March from Yorkshire and Derbyshire collieries via the G.N.&G.E. Joint line from Doncaster via Lincoln. To work this traffic the G.E. built numerous classes of 0-6-0s culminating in the large class D18, L.N.E. Class J20, built between 1920 and 1922. No.8276 is seen approaching Audley End tunnel with an up coal train. The BR classification was Class 5F. (23755)*

ABOVE : *"The Capitals Limited" was introduced by the "Fast Coast" Regions (Eastern, North Eastern and Scottish) of BR in 1949 as a summer only train non-stop between Kings Cross and Edinburgh to enable The Flying Scotsman to keep to the same schedule with the same stops in the winter and summer timetables. "The Capitals Limited" also conveyed through coaches to and from Aberdeen.*

The name of the train was changed in 1953 to "The Elizabethan" in honour of the Coronation of the Queen (A much more sensible name than something with "Coronation" in it as it does not date).

This appears to be the down train, 9.30am ex Kings Cross, as the telegraph poles were on the up side. The locomotive is (I think) 60025 "Falcon" and the photograph was probably taken in 1951 or 1952. Class B17 No. 61652 "Darlington" has just sneaked into the picture on an up Cambridge train. (2762)

ABOVE : *The pioneer Great Northern Railway Class A1, 4-6-2 No. 4470 "Great Northern" emerges from Wood Green Tunnel on a down express c. 1930. The first eleven Class A1s were built to the more generous Great Northern loading gauge with a taller chimney, dome and cab, which can be seen clearly in this picture. No. 4470 was cut down to the composite L.N.E.R. loading gauge in May 1933. Do please note the somersault distant signal on "gallows" type brackets. (410A)*

BELOW : *Digswell viaduct, Welwyn Hertfordshire crosses the valley of the River Mimram and carried its first train on Monday 5the August 1850. Various lengths have been quoted over the years but it is about 1,560 feet overall. The viaduct has forty arches each of 30 foot span and is 98 feet above the river at its maximum height. The train appears to be the down "Flying Scotsman" hauled by an unidentified Class A4 with the 1938 stock. This must have been a cloudy day otherwise, at about half past ten, E.R.Wethersett would have been shooting directly into the sun.*

LEFT, above : *Post-war austerity. A grubby Class A3 No. 62 "Minoru" passes New Southgate on a down express c.1947. The white oblong on the bridge acts as a sighting board for some up line signals to make their arms stand out against the brickwork of the bridge. (23514)*

ABOVE : *The Royal Border Bridge at Berwick upon Tweed with the down "Queen of Scots" Pullman train crossing the River Tweed. The locomotive is L.N.E.R. designed but BR built Class A1, 4-6-2 No. 60127. It was built in May 1949 and turned out in BR blue livery, as seen here, and was named "Wilson Worsdell" in September 1950. The photograph therefore must have been taken between those two dates as No. 60127 is not named. It has the original plain and ugly chimney which was later replaced by a more elegant one with a lip. The "Queen of Scots" was never a very fast train but, no doubt, it appealed to clientele who required luxury.*

There were ten cars leaving Kings Cross for Leeds where the train reversed and two carriages were detached. The train then traversed the old Leeds Northern line via Ripon re-joining the East Coast Main Line at Northallerton. (2507)

47

ABOVE : *To conclude, a view of the West Coast Main Line near Carpenders Park between Harrow and Watford. The locomotive is "Royal Scot" Class 4-6-0 No. 6144 "Honourable Artillery Company" allocated to Liverpool (Edge Hill). The train, therefore is probably a Euston to Liverpool Lime Street express, maybe the Merseyside Express, which left Euston around 6.00pm. The date of the picture is either 1935 or 1936 as the style of shed plate on the smokebox (8A = Edge Hill) was introduced in January 1935 and No. 6144 received a Stanier 4,000 gallon tender with curved sides in 1936. (926)*